Complete, Responsive Mobile App Design Using Visual Studio: Integrating MySQL Database into Your Web Page

Stephen Link

DEDICATION

This book is dedicated to my many teachers and clients over the years who have helped in the development of programming skills and flexibility in application of those skills. The logic behind those skills cannot be learned or taught. I thank God for that ingrained ability.

Complete, Responsive Mobile App Design Using Visual Studio

CONTENTS

	Acknowledgments	i
1	Explaining Current Technologies	1
2	The Project Specifications	3
3	The Login Screen	4
4	The Register Screen	9
5	The Display Screen	11
6	The Edit Screen	15
7	The About Screen	18
8	The Default Screen	20
9	Cascading Style Sheets	23
10	Brief SQL Language Explanation	25
11	The MySQL Tables	27
A	Downloading the Source	29
	About the Author	30
	Other Works	31

Complete, Responsive Mobile App Design Using Visual Studio

ACKNOWLEDGMENTS

I would like to give thanks to my God. Without Him, life would be unbearable. Thanks also to my wife who has supported me through the research and study time required to complete this book.

1 EXPLAINING CURRENT TECHNOLOGIES

HTML5, in its simplest form, is another version of the HTML specification. Previous versions would include 4.1, 3.2, and earlier. HTML stands for HyperText Markup Language. Why is version 5 so important? Because of the advances it has made in dynamic application design. Years ago web pages would tend to be static and quite boring, although they accomplished the purpose of displaying desired information. Today's web pages and apps can be designed with as much functionality as we have come to expect from stand-alone desktop applications. Incorporating video, navigation, and many other user-friendly functions on any device has become a quite normal expectation. Using HTML5 in combination with the other technologies explained in this EBook, you will acquire the ability to impress your users with the functionality that they need for everyday business functions.

CSS3 is another relatively new technology although Cascading Style Sheets have been around since 1996. As you may have guessed, CSS helps in styling and presenting your user interface. You can utilize CSS formatting within your individual HTML tags, known as in-line. You can also include a section of CSS code within the HEAD tag of your HTML page. This is known as an internal style sheet. A third way to implement cascading style sheets, and probably the most popular, is to use an external style sheet. All three methods can accomplish the same results and each has its own useful situations.

Let's say that you have a small site with only a few pages. In this case inline styling may work well. If you find that you have to apply the same styling to multiple elements, it would definitely be beneficial to use an internal style sheet. You would be able to define the style once and apply it as many times as necessary with minimal effort. Now let's carry this effort across multiple web pages and maybe even hundreds. You could define the styles in one external style sheet and include a link to it in every page. The simplicity provided by the external CSS approach is the reason for its popularity.

Javascript is a client-side language that has been around since the mid-2000s although the initial concept was known as "server side scripting" and was introduced in 1994. Now you have seen two terms which may seem contradictory - "client side" versus "server side." You probably guessed that the server, or web server, is the computer that generates the web pages that get sent to the user's computer. Good guess. The user's computer is the client; so this means that client-side processes run on the user's computer and report the results back to the server for additional processing. Any Javascript code that you write for today's systems runs as an interpreted client-side function. Oops, we threw another term out there - interpreted. The advantage of this execution methodology is that a single Javascript program can be run on many different platforms. It is loaded onto the client system and executed whether it is a Mac, PC, Linux, Android, or any number of other operating systems.

JQuery and **JQuery Mobile** (JQM) are packages that can be included into your web page or app so that you do not have to recreate the massive functionality provided by these plugins. Imagine having to chop down your own trees and mill your own lumber in order to be able to build a clubhouse. JQuery, JQM, and many other available plugins give you the ability to skip the low end function design and jump right into creativity mode. What kind of functionality? JQM is used mainly for user interface design while JQuery will allow much easier access to the components on screen. We will use both of these as the app is designed.

You may be wondering which editor you should use. Notepad will work fine if you are a hardcore HTML coder. Notepad++ works a little better than Notepad. Netbeans is my editor of choice for HTML and Java coding. Now let's hop right into the code design and explanation.

2 THE PROJECT SPECIFICATIONS

Let's start with the basic requirement to work with MySQL in Visual Studio - the connector. Take a look at http://dev.mysql.com/downloads/connector/ and what is available. Since we are working with ASP.Net web pages in Visual Studio, you should download and install "Connector/Net." Once this is installed you will be able to choose "MySQL Database" as the type of data source when setting up the new connection below.

As you have seen already, the version of Visual Studio in use is 2010 and the programming language is C#. We will start with the initial "Web Site" project view showing the selected .Net framework as 3.5. Before beginning on this project, view the Property Pages and Build window of your project to verify that you see the same Target Framework shown below.

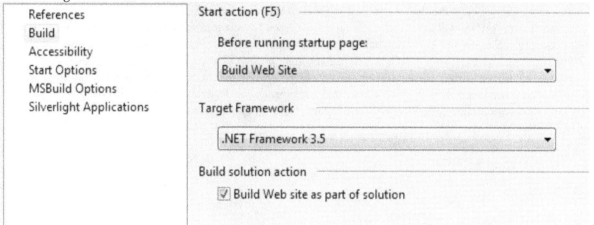

3 THE LOGIN SCREEN

We will start in the very beginning with the individual code and properties of each component in the login screen. Right-click the project-Add New Item-select "Web Form." Be sure to verify that the language selected in the left section is Visual C#. After naming the page (Login.aspx in this case) and clicking OK you will see html code. Click on the Design view (bottom of the main window) and you will see an empty <body> section.

Click "Toolbox" and choose the "Data" section. Drag SqlDataSource onto your screen. Since we only have one data source in use, the default name of "SqlDataSource1" is fine. By clicking the right-arrow on the SqlDataSource you can select "Configure Data Source" and either create a new connection (if you need one, as is the case here) or click the dropdown and select a connection from there.

As an illustration we will follow through the processes for creating a new connection. Click the "New Connection" button on the screen. Change the data source to "MySQL Database" and enter the server information received from your web host. If you set this up on your own PC you will likely use localhost and the root username and password. It is up to you if you want to check the "Save my Password" option. Although this is neither secure nor recommended for a production system, it should be okay in this learning situation. You should also select the Database name from the dropdown. Clicking Test Connection should return a "succeeded" message.

If you are developing this as a learning experience you can download MySQL and install it on your computer or use MS SQL Express if you have it already on your system. Using MSSQL Express instead of MySQL can change the SQL select statements slightly and some other approaches so a basic familiarity with SQL statements should be necessary to make that change.

Let's put the rest of the components on the login screen before proceeding. Click on Toolbox and open the "Standard" section. Drag two labels, two textboxes, and a button onto the screen above your SqlDataSource. It should look like the screen below. Are we impressed yet?

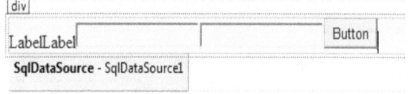

I am not too impressed since this doesn't look user friendly yet. We have the power to fix that, though, just by dragging a few things around and inserting a couple of breaks. First, put your cursor between the two labels and press <Enter> twice. You may need to select the first label and press the right arrow to get there. Now drag your first text box up one line. Do the same with the second label and textbox with a single <Enter> this time. Also insert an <Enter> between the second textbox and button. Now things look a little better but still not too impressive.

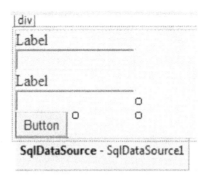

Well, we have the layout pretty decent but we need to change the item names and a few other properties to make this login screen more useful. Select the first label and change the Text to "Login Name" and the (ID) to "lblLogin" (both are without quotes). We will do the same for the second label by changing the Text to "Password" and (ID) to "lblPassword." Let's change the two textboxes to an (ID) of "txtLoginName" and "txtPassword." You should also change the TextMode to "Password" for the "txtPassword" textbox so that the characters will not be displayed when typed. Now change the text on the button to "Login" and the (ID) to "btnLogin." Do you consider this to be more user-friendly and usable?

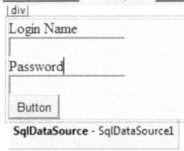

We should make this screen CSS-friendly so that we can easily apply dynamic formatting. The first step to do that is to name the div that contains the login screen. Click on the outline directly under the "div" so that the whole screen is selected. In your Properties window you should see selections for (ID), Align, Class, etc. In the (ID) block name this "divlogin." If your screen shows "div#divlogin" instead of "div" as shown above, we have finished the visual design of the login screen. We will come back to this one to apply CSS styling in a later section.

You should now be able to compile and execute this web page with no issues. If errors come up you should verify that everything has been set up exactly as previously shown. It would be nice to actually be able

to do something so we will put some code behind the "Login" button. Click the button and select Events in your Properties window. You can double-click the empty section to the right of "Click" and a window will open containing, among other text, "protected void btnLogin_Click." You should place the code shown below between the braces so that you see the following section of code (yours should be indented if typed in).

```
protected void btnLogin_Click(object sender, EventArgs e)
{
string nm;
string pwd;
DataView dv = new DataView();
DataTable dt = new DataTable();
SqlDataSource1.SelectCommand = "select * from ALogins where Username = '" +
txtLoginName.Text.Trim() + "'";
dv = (DataView)SqlDataSource1.Select(DataSourceSelectArguments.Empty);
```

```
dt = dv.ToTable();
if (dt.Rows.Count > 0)
{
nm = dv.Table.Rows[0][0].ToString();
pwd = dv.Table.Rows[0][1].ToString();
if (pwd == txtPassword.Text.Trim())
{
Session["nm"] = nm;
Server.Transfer("Display.aspx");
}
else
{
Response.Write("<script          language=javascript>alert('Incorrect          login
credentials');</script>");
Server.Transfer("Default.aspx");
}
}
else
{
nm = "Not Registered";
Response.Write("<script language=javascript>alert('" + nm + "');</script>");
Server.Transfer("Default.aspx");
}
}
```

We will go through this section of code and explain what logic is being used and why. We will also give some pointers which will work in most versions of Visual Studio. Let's clarify something about the code structure first. Do you see red underlines displayed in your code for words such as "DataView" and "DataTable?" If so, you can right-click the word, put your mouse over "Resolve" and select an option displayed. This will place a "using" statement at the top of your code and this error will disappear. Now let's get into an explanation of the code.

First we are declaring two string items at the top of our routine. This is required in the use of the C# language. We are declaring these as "string" because this is the type of data being used for these two variables as the password is retrieved from the SQL data source. Utilizing a dataview and datatable in code would seem to be the "quick and dirty" method for getting data from a datasource. That is the purpose of assigning these types in the next two lines of code.

Something to notice is that the next line of code uses "SqlDataSource1" but we have not defined this in our code. SqlDataSource1 refers to the SqlDataSource that we created in design view above. By setting the SelectCommand to what you see here we are getting only the name and password from the ALogins table in our database. We then assign the data into the currently empty DataView (dv) that we have assigned at the top of our routine. The "(DataView)" statement is required in front of the SqlDataSource1.Select command because we are retrieving a dataset which is then converted to a dataview. Another requirement is the presence of "DataSourceSelectArguments.Empty" because we have already set the SelectCommand. We will use ToTable() method to convert our retrieved results from a dataview to datatable so that we can check for results and cycle through them.

By checking dt.rows.count we can verify that a correct username was entered. If not we fall through to the "Not Registered" message and transfer back to the Default page. Otherwise we can check the password against what was entered. We set "nm" equal to the username that was retrieved (first row, first field of our table) and "pwd" is set to the password retrieved (first row, second field). By determining that pwd and the entry into the txtPassword box are equal we can set a "required" session variable and move on to the Display page for entering mileage and viewing location information. If an incorrect password was entered we display the "Incorrect login credentials" message and redirect to Default.

4 THE REGISTER SCREEN

Just as you did before, add a new web form and name it "Register.aspx." You will also add a SqlDataSource just as you did for the Login screen. We will name it "dbconn" by changing the (ID) property. This screen will have five labels, three textboxes, and a button. Separate those just like you did previously with the press of the <Enter> key.

```
div
You will be allowed to select your own login name and password
Username

Password

We collect email addresses for additional walkthe... notifications. You will not be contacted for any other reason unless specifically requested
Email Address

Register
SqlDataSource - dbconn
```

The screen should look as above and the component names, top to bottom, are lblLogin, lblUsername, txtUsername, lblPassword, txtPassword, lblMessage, lblEmail, txtEmail, and btnRegister. You should change the TextMode to "Password" for the txtPassword TextBox. Notice that we did not give this div its own name. As before, the only component on this screen that has code is btnRegister. Double-click on the Click event as you did on the previous screen. That code is shown below.

```
protected void btnRegister_Click(object sender, EventArgs e)
{
DataView dv = new DataView();
DataTable dt = new DataTable();
dbconn.SelectCommand = "select Username from ALogins where Username = '" +
txtUsername.Text.Trim() + "'";
dv = (DataView)dbconn.Select(DataSourceSelectArguments.Empty);
dt = dv.ToTable();
if (dt.Rows.Count > 0)
{
Response.Write("<script language=javascript>alert('That username is already
taken');</script>");
```

```
    txtUsername.Focus();
    }
    else
    {
    dbconn.InsertCommand  =  "insert  into  ALogins  (Username,pwd,email)  values  ('"  +
txtUsername.Text.Trim()  +  "','"  +  txtpwd.Text.Trim()  +  "','"  +  txtemail.Text.Trim()  +
"')";
    dbconn.Insert();
    Session["nm"] = txtUsername.Text.Trim();
    Server.Transfer("Display.aspx");
    }
    }
```

You will notice that we are using the same basic function as before to load the username from our database and convert the results to a datatable. The purpose of this is to check if the username entered already exists. Therefore, we check for rows.count > 0 and display a message that the username already exists and send the focus back to the username field. If the username does not exist we fall through to a section of code which builds an insert command, executes it on the database, assigns a required session variable, and transfers to the display screen.

You will notice that the insert command is inserting into the ALogins table of our database and it is assigning three fields (username, pwd, email) with the three values that were typed into this screen. The command that actually executes that command is dbconn.Insert(). The next line assigns a "required" session variable, as mentioned previously. Why is it required? This web page does not require it and Visual Studio doesn't either, but the Display.aspx page checks for that session variable and will redirect to the Default page if it is not found. This requirement is a minimal security maneuver although it will not keep out a determined hacker.

5 THE DISPLAY SCREEN

You have seen a couple of screens that are rather simple in design and functionality. Now you get to work with a page that is more detailed in design, contains a hyperlink, a calendar control, and it even utilizes two SqlDataSources. That would be the screen that functions as our data entry and information display. Create a new web form in the same fashion as before and name it "Display.aspx." On this screen you will add 11 labels, one hyperlink, one Calendar (both are in the Standard section), one textbox, three buttons, and two SqlDataSources. You can design the screen to look like the screen shot below.

[div]

Your current location is:
Mileage: [lblMileage]
Location: [lblLocation]
Elevation: [lblElevation]
County/State: [lblCountyST]
Long/Lat [lblLongLat]
HyperLink

<			February 2014			>
Sun	**Mon**	**Tue**	**Wed**	**Thu**	**Fri**	**Sat**
26	27	28	29	30	31	1
2	3	4	5	6	7	8
9	10	11	12	13	14	15
16	17	18	19	20	21	22
23	24	25	26	27	28	1
2	3	4	5	6	7	8

[ ] Insert Mileage

Edit my mileage

Logout

SqlDataSource - dbconn

SqlDataSource - dbMileage

The names, top to bottom and left to right, are lblCurrloc, lblMileage0, lblMileage, lblLocation0, lblLocation, lblElevation0, lblElevation, lblCountyST0, lblCountyST, lblLongLat0, lblLongLat, lnkPicture, calMileage, txtMileage, btnInsert, btnEdit, btnLogout, dbconn, and dbmileage. You should set the Text property for the buttons as they are shown. The width of calMileage should be set to 75%. Now we will look at the code that drives the page. Let's start with a couple of globally assigned variables and the Page_Load function. What is Page_Load? As you may have guessed from the name, it is executed when the page is loaded from the web server. That section of code is shown below.

```
string uname;
double currttl;
protected void Page_Load(object sender, EventArgs e)
{
if (Session["nm"] == null)
{
Server.Transfer("Default.aspx");
}
else
{
uname = Session["nm"].ToString();
if (!IsPostBack)
{
DateTime currdt = DateTime.Today;
calMileage.TodaysDate = currdt;
calMileage.SelectedDate = calMileage.TodaysDate;
}
DataView dv = new DataView();
DataTable dt = new DataTable();
DataView dv2 = new DataView();
DataTable dt2 = new DataTable();
dbconn.SelectCommand = "select * from AEntries where Username = '" + uname + "' order
by id";
dv = (DataView)dbconn.Select(DataSourceSelectArguments.Empty);
dt = dv.ToTable();
if (dt.Rows.Count > 0)
{
currttl = Convert.ToDouble(dv.Table.Rows[dt.Rows.Count-1][4].ToString());
DateTime        currdt        =        Convert.ToDateTime(dv.Table.Rows[dt.Rows.Count        -
1][2].ToString()).AddDays(1);
if (!IsPostBack)
{
calMileage.TodaysDate = currdt;
calMileage.SelectedDate = calMileage.TodaysDate;
}
dbMileage.SelectCommand = "select * from AMileage where Distance >= " + currttl + "
limit 1";
dv2 = (DataView)dbMileage.Select(DataSourceSelectArguments.Empty);
dt2 = dv2.ToTable();
lblMileage.Text = currttl.ToString();
lblLocation.Text = dt2.Rows[0][1].ToString();
lblElevation.Text = dt2.Rows[0][2].ToString();
lblCountyST.Text = dt2.Rows[0][4].ToString() + "/" + dt2.Rows[0][3].ToString();
lblLongLat.Text = dt2.Rows[0][5].ToString() + "/" + dt2.Rows[0][6].ToString();
if (dt2.Rows[0][7].ToString() != "")
{
lnkPicture.Text = "View Picture";
lnkPicture.NavigateUrl = dt2.Rows[0][7].ToString();
}
else
```

```
    {
    lnkPicture.Visible = false;
    }
    }
    }
```

Lots of code! It would seem that way compared to the snippets shown so far. Keep in mind, though, that this is only one function out of quite a few on this page. But what does it do? Basically, it loads and displays the current location of the user who has logged in. Do you remember that "required" session variable that was set in the previous two screens? That was assigning the name of the logged in user to a session variable that is maintained throughout the currently logged in web session. If it has not been assigned (equal to null) the program will redirect to the Default page. Otherwise it will continue to load and display the current information that matches the mileage.

Now that we have verified that the session variable exists we can set a variable called "uname." You may be wondering about the "if (!IsPostBack)" statement. That handles the current page so that it will only execute the code inside of the braces on the initial page load. Now let's look at the function of that block of code. The first line sets up a datetime variable called currdt equal to today. Then we set the calendar date and selected date to today. This is done to make it easier on the user who wants to make daily entries into the mileage log. Because it only executes on the first page load, the date does not reset to today after every mileage entry.

You should be familiar with the approach of loading the data from our database. Although we set up the dataview, datatable, and select command in a quite similar fashion; the processing becomes a bit more complicated after verifying that we have loaded mileage data from the AEntries table for the current user. We are able to determine the current mileage by pulling the value of the last row and field number 4. We do a conversion to double numeric format because that will give us the precision desired for calculation. Our next line of code sets the variable currdt to the last entry date plus one day (field number 2). We convert that to a datetime so that we can use AddDays(1) to increment the day on the calendar. We again check for !IsPostBack and change the calendar date if this is the first page load.

Now we get to use the dbMileage SqlDataSource to determine the next location details based on the current mileage. To get the next point we select from AMileage where Distance is greater than or equal to (>=) the current mileage total and limit it to only one row. By doing this we are guaranteed to get a row unless the current mileage is beyond our last point. We read the data and convert it to a table using the same process as other routines. Each field is then assigned to its location on screen (location, elevation, county/state, long/lat) and the code then looks at the picture hyperlink field to verify that it is not empty. As long as it is populated, the user will see a label of "View Picture" and the target URL is the link (column 7) pulled from the AMileage table. If the picture URL is empty the hyperlink control is hidden.

The code for the Click event of btnInsert is rather simple. It will create a string variable called seldt. The next step is to verify that something was entered into the txtMileage TextBox and it is numeric. We are using a function aptly titled isNumeric (covered next) that returns T or F. If there is a numeric entry into txtMileage then we will convert it to double before adding it to currttl. The next line of code reads the selected date from the calendar control and assigns it to seldt. The next two lines create and execute an insert command to add the new entry into AEntries for the username. Did you wonder how we were able to load in the last entry for the user and determine the mileage total? The answer to that pondering would be contained here also - each line contains a current total entry. The final two lines reset the txtMileage field and reload the Display screen.

You may have wondered how the IsPostBack tests work. When we reload the page from itself as we do here, it is considered a postback. Therefore the two IF statements in the Page_Load section of code that check for !IsPostBack (is not a postback) will not execute their code section because this load is considered a postback.

```
    protected void btnInsert_Click(object sender, EventArgs e)
    {
    string seldt;
```

```
if              (txtMileage.Text.Length              >              0              &&
isNumeric(txtMileage.Text,System.Globalization.NumberStyles.Number))
   {
   currttl = currttl + Convert.ToDouble(txtMileage.Text);
   seldt       =        calMileage.SelectedDate.Year.ToString()        +        "-"        +
calMileage.SelectedDate.Month.ToString() + "-" + calMileage.SelectedDate.Day.ToString();
   dbconn.InsertCommand = "insert into AEntries (Username,Dateent,entry,currttl) values
('" + uname + "','" + seldt + "'," + txtMileage.Text + "," + currttl + ")";
   dbconn.Insert();
   txtMileage.Text = "";
   Server.Transfer("Display.aspx");
   }
   }
```

The isNumeric function is rather small in lines of code but not so simple in functionality.
```
public bool isNumeric(string val, System.Globalization.NumberStyles NumberStyle)
{
Double result;
return Double.TryParse(val, NumberStyle,
System.Globalization.CultureInfo.CurrentCulture, out result);
}
```

This is a public function that returns a Boolean and accepts a string and numberstyle as parameters. The only real processing done by this function is performed by the TryParse command. It will look at a string (val) and try to convert it to the numeric precision indicated (Double) using the indicated numberstyle. Although the numeric result of the conversion (or 0) is placed in the result parameter, we are interested in the return of T if the conversion was successful or F if not.

The code placed in the Click event of btnEdit is really simple since the only thing that it does is transfer to the Edit.aspx page. The btnLogout Click event is just as simple in transferring back to the Default page.
```
protected void btnEdit_Click(object sender, EventArgs e)
{
Server.Transfer("Edit.aspx");
}

protected void btnLogout_Click(object sender, EventArgs e)
{
Server.Transfer("Default.aspx");
}
```

6 THE EDIT SCREEN

Add another web form to your project and call it Edit.aspx. This form is rather simple in its design because it only contains a gridview, button and SqlDataSource.

div		
	dateent	entry
Edit Delete	2/11/2014	0
Edit Delete	2/11/2014	0.1
Edit Delete	2/11/2014	0.2
Edit Delete	2/11/2014	0.3
Edit Delete	2/11/2014	0.4
Edit Delete	2/11/2014	0.5
Edit Delete	2/11/2014	0.6
Edit Delete	2/11/2014	0.7
Edit Delete	2/11/2014	0.8
Edit Delete	2/11/2014	0.9
1 2		

Return

SqlDataSource - SqlDataSource1

Gridview is located in the Data section of your Toolbox. Arrange your form to look like the screen shot shown above. The Gridview width should be set to 75% and the DataSourceID is SqlDataSource1. Set the DataKeyNames to id. With the GridView selected you will notice a "right-arrow" button in the upper right corner. You can click that and check "Enable Editing" and "Enable Deleting" to display the links shown in the left column. Name the button btnReturn. Now let's get to the code since it is not so simple.

Click on the Gridview to select it and then click on the ellipsis for the Columns property. Select the id field in the "Selected fields" section, drag the selector bar down, and you will get a screen similar to the one below.

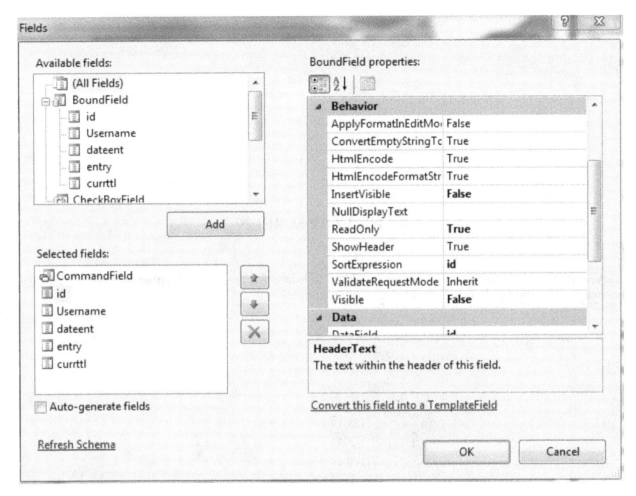

Notice that Visible for the id field is set to false. The Username and currttl fields should also be set to Visible = False. This will display the only fields that need to be viewed and edited.

Unlike the Page_Load on the Display page, this page load section of code is rather simple. We start, as before, by defining a global "uname" variable. Then we check for the assigned session variable and head back to the Default page if it is not populated. Next we assign the "uname" variable and select all entries (AEntries table) into SqlDataSource1 for that user. We set the order to id on that statement so that we retrieve the most recent entry last.

```
string uname;
protected void Page_Load(object sender, EventArgs e)
{
if (Session["nm"] == null)
{
Server.Transfer("Default.aspx");
}
else
{
uname = Session["nm"].ToString();
SqlDataSource1.SelectCommand = "select * from AEntries where Username = '" + uname +
"' order by id";
SqlDataSource1.Select(DataSourceSelectArguments.Empty);
}
```

```
        }
```

The one button on this page is also quite simple in its processing. It will select all entries for the current username and then set the total mileage on all of them to the current total. Keep in mind that you are editing or deleting the mileage here. Instead of trying to determine the current edit spot and adjusting only the entries following it, all totals are changed. These are changed using the update statement shown inside of the "IF" statement.

```
protected void btnReturn_Click(object sender, EventArgs e)
{
// cycle through SQLDataSource1 and total entry as cttl
double cttl=0;
DataView dv = new DataView();
DataTable dt = new DataTable();
DataView dv2 = new DataView();
SqlDataSource1.SelectCommand = "select sum(entry) from AEntries where Username = '" +
uname + "'";
dv = (DataView)SqlDataSource1.Select(DataSourceSelectArguments.Empty);
dt = dv.ToTable();
if (dt.Rows.Count > 0)
{
cttl = Convert.ToDouble(dv.Table.Rows[0][0].ToString());
SqlDataSource1.UpdateCommand = "update AEntries as t1 set t1.currttl = " + cttl + "
where Username = '" + uname + "'";
SqlDataSource1.Update();
}
Server.Transfer("Display.aspx");
}
```

The major functionality of this page is editing the data. You actually do not have to enter code to accomplish this because it is performed automatically by the Gridview edit and delete functions. This is possible because custom SQL statements were entered into SqlDataSource1. Put your mouse over the datasource, click on the right arrow, and choose the "Configure …" option. Click Next and verify that "Specify a custom SQL statement …" is selected and then click Next. For the SELECT statement you will enter " SELECT * FROM AEntries." The UPDATE statement will be " update AEntries set entry=@entry where id=@id." The DELETE statement will be " delete from AEntries where id=@id." Since we are not inserting from this control you can leave that statement blank.

Now let's have a little explanation of those SQL statements. This varies somewhat from the SQL statements used in the code because it is customized for the Gridview operations. Above you saw that the id field is included in the Gridview even though it is not visible. This field is unique for each row so that is what is used in the WHERE clause for updating or deleting entries. This is seen in the SQL statements as "@id." The field shown as "@entry" refers to the entry field displayed on screen in the rightmost column.

7 THE ABOUT SCREEN

This is an important page for any app that you design. You can use this location to showcase your business, capabilities, and anything else that you may want to place there. You should also include user instructions here, of course. This is a quite simple design with any number of labels, links, and a "Return" button. The About page for this app is shown below.

|div|

We at LinkEmUp hope that you enjoy your exercise experience. This was designed to encourage you in walking, running, cycling, or whatever form of exercise is most productive for you. This is a free offering and you are encouraged to spread the word among your friends as we all focus on becoming healthier Americans.

We also want to introduce you and your business associates to the large number of services that we offer. You will see web design, custom programming, and even training by visiting the <u>Link Em Up web site</u>

When you register for the free login we request your email address only so that we can notify you of any additional Walkthe... offerings that may be coming later. If we get a large amount of participation we may be able to offer pictorial views of the American Discovery Trail, Buckeye Trail, and others. You will not be contacted regarding our business services unless you specifically request that information. The information used here was gathered from various web sites but the main two are summitpost.org and wikipedia.org. As you will notice, the pictures shown also span many web sites.

Usage Instructions

If you have not previously registered that should be your first step. When you register you can choose a username and password. We ask for your email address only to send alerts of anything that may be happening with this application or alert you of similar "walk the ..." applications as they become available. Click Register once this info has been entered.

If you have already registered you should login at the initial screen. Enter your username and password to continue. After logging in you will see information about your current location. To insert a new entry select the correct date, enter the mileage, and click or tap "Insert Mileage." If you have a need to edit the mileage you will use the "Edit my mileage" button. When editing mileage select the page where the desired entry resides (page numbers shown below data) and click or tap "Edit" beside the entry that you want to edit. Change the number, click or tap Update, and then click or tap the "Return" button.

Return

You may be thinking "I don't need a bunch of labels, I can accomplish that by just typing the text on the page." You would be correct in that thinking. You would also have trouble working with the individual formatting of each section if that is desired. When we get to the CSS section you will see how much power and flexibility is available through the use of Cascading Style Sheets.

8 THE DEFAULT SCREEN

You have heard quite a bit about returning to the Default screen. That would be Default.aspx which functions as the home page for our app. It was saved as the last screen since it is the driver for others. The home page for this app has a waterfall picture that was taken from the content of the program along with a few other buttons. The screen is shown below.

The image width is set to 95% so that it will scale to the device size. You have seen the target page for all of these buttons other than "Visit our Forums." This is actually hosted in a forums app so that functionality will not be covered in detail. The first three navigation buttons are simple page transfers and they are shown below. You have seen the individual pages and their functionality in earlier sections.

```
protected void btnLogin_Click(object sender, EventArgs e)
{
Server.Transfer("Login.aspx");
}
protected void Button1_Click(object sender, EventArgs e)
{
Server.Transfer("About.aspx");
}
protected void btnRegister_Click(object sender, EventArgs e)
{
Server.Transfer("Register.aspx");
}
```

We will cover the code of the Forums button due to the variation in its approach. When someone chooses to go outside of our main site we want to open the destination in a new window. This is handled through a small javascript block. We set the destination URL and create a new Stringbuilder variable (sb). Inside of this variable we build a javascript function which opens a new browser window and loads the web site specified in the "url" variable. By paying close attention to the code you will see that there is actually only one line between the opening and closing "script" tags.

```csharp
protected void btnForum_Click(object sender, EventArgs e)
{
string url = "http://forums.linkemup.us";
StringBuilder sb = new StringBuilder();
sb.Append("<script type = 'text/javascript'>");
sb.Append("window.open('");
sb.Append(url);
sb.Append("');");
sb.Append("</script>");
ClientScript.RegisterStartupScript(this.GetType(),"script", sb.ToString());
}
```

That single line will appear as "window.open('http://forums.linkemup.us');" After this the final line of code will register and execute that script.

9 CASCADING STYLE SHEETS

So far we have a functioning app, although it is somewhat plain. We can easily change the appearance of our app and add a background picture along with colors to the buttons. The big consideration for today's app design is mentioned in the title of this EBook - Responsive. So far we have done nothing that will make this app responsive to various devices and platforms. This is another capability added through CSS design. Take a look at the CSS sheet below. It was added into our project and dragged onto each sheet to be made available.

```css
body
{
}

@media all and (min-width: 800px)
{
.divlogin,buttonplace
{
font-family: sans-serif;
font-size: 25px;
color: black;
text-align: left;
}
.textfont
{
font-size:30px;
}
.buttonplace
{
float:left;
background-color:Teal;
}
}
@media all and (min-width: 350px) and (max-width: 799px)
{
.divlogin,buttonplace
{
font-family: sans-serif;
font-size: 30px;
color: black;
text-align: left;
}
```

```
.textfont
{
font-size:35px;
}
.buttonplace
{
float:left;
background-color:Teal;
}
}
@media all and (max-width: 349px)
{
.divlogin,buttonplace
{
font-family: sans-serif;
font-size: 40px;
color: black;
text-align: left;
}
.textfont
{
font-size:45px;
}
.buttonplace
{
float:left;
background-color:Teal;
}
}
```

Now let's have an explanation of the formatting and application advice. Notice the three "@media all and ..." sections. This is how we handle responsiveness and resizing based on the viewport size. As you can tell from the code, it will use one section for 800px or greater width. The second section will be applied with a viewport width from 350 to 799px and the third will apply to a smaller viewport.

We will only go through one section since they are similar in design although the sizing is adjusted. The ".divlogin" selection applies to all components that have been assigned the "divlogin" class. You should also notice that "buttonplace" is assigned here after a comma in addition to being assigned below in its own section. This is acceptable and works to combine aspects from each section where the name is included. The font size, type, color, and alignment are defined here. Font size will change based on the viewport size. After combining this with "buttonplace" there is no need to use the "divlogin" class for the screen components.

The ".textfont" class assigns the font size based on viewport size. In design mode for each screen you should assign each of your TextBoxes and Labels to have this class using the "CssClass" property.

The "buttonplace" class assigns a float left property and a background color. These are combined with the properties assigned above in the "divlogin" section. Assign the CssClass of "buttonplace" to all of the buttons in the app.

In order to add a little more pizazz to the app we can download a background image to use on all of our pages. Since this app is based on the idea of "Walk the Appalachian Trail" I chose "autumn leaves jpg" and placed that in the "Background" property (under DOCUMENT) for each of the pages created.

In this somewhat simplified layout and formatting, we have done very little with the CSS creation and layouts. You could choose to apply this capability and make a beautifully flowing app with additional viewport formats accounted for. You could also apply different formatting and sizing for some buttons, text, and other components. How deeply CSS formatting is applied is completely up to your imagination.

10 BRIEF SQL LANGUAGE EXPLANATION

You have seen Select, Update, and Insert SQL statements used in the procedures of this app. Let's first cover the approach of selecting data that was used many times in the preceding sections.

The SELECT statement performs the exact functionality that you would expect based on the name - it selects data from a table. Take a look at one of the select statements pulled from the app that we have been examining.

```
select sum(entry) from AEntries where Username = '" + uname + "'"
```

We actually have a little more than just a plain select statement here. First we see "sum(entry)" which means that the sum of the entry field is returned from the AEntries table. We also see a where clause that selects only the data for the current username stored in the "uname" variable. Also notice the single quote (') character which is on both sides of that variable. That is required because this is a string element in the table. If the data was numeric we would not need, or be able to use, the quote characters. Microsoft SQL, also known as Transact SQL or T-SQL, would use the exact same wording and approach for such a simple select statement.

Now we will look at a select statement that becomes a little more complicated by adding an "order by" clause at the end.

```
select * from AEntries where Username = '" + uname + "' order by id"
```

In this statement we have the same basic structure as before other than the use of "*" to select all fields and the absence of sum applied. At the end we have an "order by id" statement added. This determines how the data will be sorted. Because we have an automatically generated number as id in our AEntries table the data returned will be in chronological (entered) order. In this app the above statement works well for looking at the last entry to determine the current mileage of the user. T-SQL will also use the same format for this select command.

Let's take a look at an UPDATE statement next.

```
"update AEntries as t1 set t1.currttl = "+cttl+" where Username = '"+uname+"'"
```

In this statement you see a rather simple MySQL update statement. The first entry shown after the update command is the table to be updated, AEntries in this case. Next, in order to simplify the statement, we assign it a short and simple table alias (as t1). Why do we do this? In this statement with only one table it may not make a huge difference. If we had four or five lengthy table names this could shorten the code tremendously. Following this we set a specific field to the value of the variable being assigned to it. Notice that there are no quote (') characters around this variable name. This works because it is a numeric field. You see the where clause that has become quite familiar.

Since we are comparing T-SQL code, let's look at the same code in that format and then without the table alias.

```
"update AEntries t1 set t1.currttl = "+cttl+" where Username = '"+uname+"'"
```

As you can see, not much has changed although the T-SQL syntax does not support AS between the table name and alias. What difference would it make if the table alias were removed? See the statement below for than answer.

```
"update AEntries set AEntries.currttl = "+cttl+" where AEntries.Username = '"+uname+"'"
```

Now let's move on to an INSERT statement which is a bit more complicated than the two previously shown. In this case we are inserting into the ALogins table.

```
"insert into ALogins (Username,pwd,email) values ('" + txtUsername.Text.Trim() + "','" + txtpwd.Text.Trim() + "','" + txtemail.Text.Trim() + "')"
```

Following the table name, with the parentheses, are the three fields that we are inserting into. After that we have the "values" keyword followed by another opening parentheses and a quote character ('). Behind that we are appending the field names from our page that contains the values to insert. Each field is surrounded by a quote (') character since it is a character field. Finally we close the statement with the closing parentheses character. Creating this command for T-SQL would use the exact same code and formatting.

11 THE MYSQL TABLES

Although you can download the sample project for this app (whew, I thought I was going to have to type all of that!), you will have to design your own database and tables. The data below will give all information needed to complete that task in MySQL.

	Field	Type	Collation	Attributes	Null	Default	Extra
☐	id	bigint(15)			No		auto_increment
☐	Username	varchar(10)	utf8_general_ci		No		
☐	dateent	date			No		
☐	entry	decimal(5,2)			No		
☐	currttl	decimal(10,2)			No		

The database name used for my database is "ATWalking" and this is the table named "AEntries." This shows the auto_increment "id" field which helps us to sort by that field to determine the latest entry. Just in case you are wondering, the server name is blacked out for security purposes. Next we have the ALogins table.

Field	Type	Collation	Attributes	Null	Default	Extra
Username	varchar(10)	utf8_general_ci		No		
pwd	varchar(10)	utf8_general_ci		No		
email	varchar(75)	utf8_general_ci		Yes	NULL	

You may notice something a little different here, other than the default collation setting for character fields - the Null and Default settings that are used for email. If you have Null set to No, as it has been until this field, the field cannot be blank. If something goes wrong and that field is not populated when trying to write to the table (update or insert) the process will error out and the data will not be saved. With this set to Yes as it is with email, the field is optional and there are no problems if it is left blank. Now on to the all-important AMileage table.

Field	Type	Collation	Attributes	Null	Default	Extra
Distance	decimal(10,2)			No		
Feature	varchar(75)	utf8_general_ci		No		
Elevation	smallint(4)			Yes	NULL	
State	varchar(2)	utf8_general_ci		Yes	NULL	
County	varchar(20)	utf8_general_ci		Yes	NULL	
Long	decimal(10,4)			Yes	NULL	
Lat	decimal(10,4)			Yes	NULL	
Picture	varchar(150)	utf8_general_ci		Yes	NULL	

This is actually the table that drives this app. The data was gathered from various sources across the web including summitpost.org, Wikipedia, Whiteblaze.net, and many sites where those with enough stamina have hiked the AT and posted pictures for others to behold. You are free to design the table and fill it with whatever data you see fit.

This app was up and running beautifully at my site, linkemup.us, at the time of this writing. My domain name has been switched since, and the ASP.Net site designed here is no longer functional. It has been re-written using custom WordPress programming and an eBook will soon be available detailing the processes and accomplishments of that adventure.

APPENDIX A

You can download a zip file with complete source code for the app designed in this EBook. The datasource connection will be blank so you will need to create your own database and fill the details before being able to execute the app. The download location is

https://wwwords.biz/bookfiles/VSBook.zip

My company web site should you be interested in business services and other offerings by Link Em Up can be found at https://wwwords.biz

You should note that running the supplied code on your local desktop system can be inconsistent whether using Firefox or Chrome browsers. It has executed properly before on my desktop system from the hard drive using Firefox. The app executes perfectly from a web location, though, across many different platforms. It is also possible to utilize this code coupled with a program such as Phonegap and create a stand-alone app for the iPhone or Android. There is a suggestion which can result in an extremely beneficial learning experience for you as a programmer and also benefit a local organization. Contact a local hospital, wilderness learning center, or maybe even a boy scout troop and suggest that they be the recipient of the output from your experiment. This will give some motivation beyond just trudging through the pages of a book and will give opportunities to customize and improve upon the code presented here.

ABOUT THE AUTHOR

Stephen J. Link is a "computer guy" by profession, an author by hobby, and a Layman in the study of God's Word. He has a computer support book entitled "Link Em Up On Outlook" that was published in 2004 as a paperback (renamed to "Power Outlook" in reprint). He also has over 125 articles covering various topics published on his own blog and independent sites. Various Books have been published covering a number of topics. As a programmer, he has a unique approach to help you master the ability to create the code for automating processes and adding efficiency to your client's or employer's processes.

OTHER WORKS BY STEPHEN LINK AND
LINK EM UP, PUBLISHING DIVISION

Programming and Design

HTML5, CSS3, Javascript and JQuery Mobile Programming: Beginning to End Cross-Platform App Design

Complete, Responsive, Mobile App Design Using Visual Studio: Integrating MySQL Database into your web page

Four Programming Languages Creating a Complete Webscraper Application

Excel Programming through VBA: A Complete Macro Driven Excel 2010 Application

Christian Study

The Journey Along God's Road to Revelation: Complete Scripture Reading in a Year

Volume 1 of the Potter's Clay series: Mold Your Spirit with a Study in Proverbs

Volume 2 of the Potter's Clay series: Mold Your Spirit with a Study in Matthew

Volume 3 of the Potter's Clay series: Mold Your Spirit with a Study in John

Volume 4 of the Potter's Clay series: Mold Your Spirit with another Study in John

Volume 5 of the Potter's Clay series: Mold Your Spirit with a Study in Hebrews

Volume 6 of the Potter's Clay series: Mold Your Spirit with a Study in Acts

Your Computer

Control Your Windows 7 View: Use a Single Wallpaper Across All of Your Screens

Most are in Ebook format and are available across multiple platforms. You can start at https://wwwords.biz to select the book and platform needed. As time allows, these books will be made available for purchase in print.

Social connections

www.facebook.com/stephen.linkemup

www.twitter.com/slinkemup

www.linkedin.com/in/slinkemup